HALLOWEEN

Gooseberry Patch Co.

Packed with easy tips and ideas plus fun recipes & crafts to make your season sp**oo**ky.

What's Inside...

Light the way to your haunted house...wind twinkling lights of orange and white through the trees, bushes and around the porch railings!

Deviled Bat Wings

Stretch out the wings on the baking pan...they'll look just like bat wings when roasted!

3 lbs. whole chicken wings
1/2 c. honey
1/3 c. soy sauce
2 T. chili sauce
2 T. oil

2 t. salt
1 t. garlic powder
1 t. Worcestershire sauce
1/2 t. ground ginger

Place wings in a large plastic zipping bag. In a saucepan over low heat, stir remaining ingredients until blended; cool. Pour marinade into bag; seal and turn to coat. Refrigerate at least 8 hours. Drain wings, discarding marinade; arrange in a greased jelly-roll pan. Bake, uncovered, at 375 degrees for 30 minutes. Drain; turn wings and bake an additional 20 to 25 minutes, until glaze is set and juices run clear. Makes 12 to 15 servings.

Moldy Cheese Spread

Pop the jar into a replica paper maché Jack-'O-Lantern basket for a welcome "ghostess" gift!

1 c. crumbled blue cheese
8-oz. pkg. cream cheese, softened
3 T. mayonnaise
1 t. Worcestershire sauce

1 t. garlic salt
1 t. paprika
Optional: 1 T. sherry or cognac

Combine all ingredients in a mixing bowl; blend well. Pack in a covered jar or crock; refrigerate for several days to allow flavors to blend. Keep refrigerated. Makes about 2 cups.

Candy Corn Pizza

Pizza wedges look like pieces of candy corn!

12-inch Italian pizza crust
1 c. pizza sauce
1/3 c. shredded mozzarella cheese

3/4 c. shredded Cheddar cheese
1 c. shredded Monterey
  Jack cheese

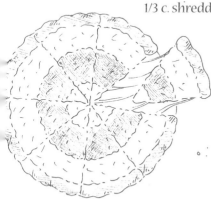

Place pizza crust on a 12" pizza pan; spread evenly with sauce. Sprinkle mozzarella cheese in center of pizza; sprinkle Cheddar and Monterey Jack cheeses in rings around mozzarella. Bake at 450 degrees for 10 to 15 minutes, until cheese is melted and crust is golden. Slice into wedges. Makes 6 servings.

Old Bones & Dracula Dip

No bones about it...these bread sticks are tasty!

7-oz. can refrigerated bread stick dough
1 egg white, beaten
1 T. grated Parmesan cheese

1/2 t. dried basil
Garnish: 8-oz. can pizza sauce, warmed

Unroll dough and separate into 6 strips; roll each between hands to 12-inches long. Tie both ends of each strip in a loose knot. Arrange on an ungreased baking sheet. Brush with egg white; sprinkle with Parmesan and basil. Bake at 375 degrees for 12 to 14 minutes, until golden. Serve with warm sauce for dipping. Makes 6.

Give the kids a box of glow-in-the-dark chalk and send 'em out to decorate the walk. "Enter If You Dare...Go Back Now...You've Been Warned... EEK!"

3

Set out a
"ghost" book
for everyone
to sign as
they arrive.
Label a blank
book
"FAMILY &
FIENDS" in
spooky
lettering...
set out a
plumed pen
and a pot of
blood-red ink
for signing.

Ghoulish Guacamole

*Garnish with a spooky spider web! Fill a small plastic zipping bag with
sour cream, snip off a corner and pipe a spiral on the guacamole. Draw
a knife tip through it to form a "web." Plastic spiders are optional!*

3 avocados, pitted and peeled
juice of 1 lime
1/2 t. salt
2 roma tomatoes, diced

1/2 c. onion, diced
3 T. fresh cilantro, chopped
1 t. garlic, minced
blue tortilla chips

Mash together avocados, lime juice and salt. Stir in
tomatoes, onion, cilantro and garlic. Chill for one
hour before serving. Serve with tortilla chips.
Makes about 3 cups.

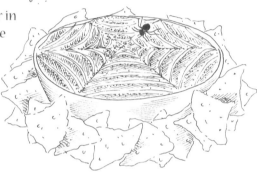

Crispy Caterpillars

*Spear with extra-long picks...poke the other end of the picks into a
brightly colored squash or gourd.*

14-oz. pkg. mini smoked sausages
1 lb. bacon, sliced into thirds

3/4 c. brown sugar, packed

Wrap each sausage in a strip of bacon; roll in
brown sugar. Fasten with toothpicks;
arrange on a lightly greased baking
sheet. Bake at 325 degrees for
40 minutes, until sugar is bubbly.
Makes 16 servings.

Creepy Cheese Eyeballs

Here's looking at you!

6-oz. jar macadamia nuts
8-oz. pkg. cream cheese, softened
3/4 c. finely shredded Cheddar cheese
2 t. lemon juice
1/8 t. garlic salt
1/8 t. pepper
Optional: 1/8 t. cayenne pepper
Garnish: sliced green or black olives

Finely chop nuts in a food processor. Measure 1/3 cup and return to food processor; set aside remaining chopped nuts on a small plate. Add remaining ingredients except olives to food processor; process until smooth. Cover and chill for one hour. Shape into balls by 2 teaspoonfuls; roll in reserved chopped nuts on plate. Press an olive slice onto each ball. Makes about 3 dozen.

Fright Night Fondue

Keep this scrumptious dip warm in a mini slow cooker.

2 c. apple cider
2 c. shredded mozzarella cheese
1-1/2 c. shredded provolone cheese
1/4 c. all-purpose flour
1/2 t. garlic powder
1/4 t. onion powder
assorted crackers, sliced bread or vegetables

In a medium saucepan over medium heat, bring cider to a boil. Simmer until reduced to one cup. Add remaining ingredients; mix well. Cook and stir until bubbly and cheese melts; whisk until smooth. Serve immediately with crackers, bread or veggies for dipping. Makes about 5 cups.

A Halloween Riddle...

Q: Why did the monster eat a light bulb?

A: Because he just wanted a light snack!

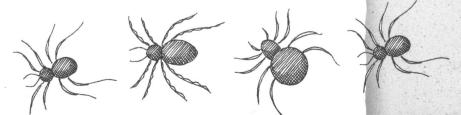

Spooky Starters

Glass bottles of soda are party-perfect... choose flavors in seasonal colors like red, orange, green and purple. Print up some scary new labels with names like "Bat's Blood" and "Swamp Juice" to tape onto bottles.

Pumpkin Brains

Serve this sweet, creamy dip in a bowl set inside a carved Jack-'O-Lantern...brave guests can dip directly from his head!

2 8-oz. pkgs. cream cheese, softened
4 c. powdered sugar
30-oz. can pumpkin pie filling

2 t. cinnamon
2 t. ground ginger
gingersnaps, vanilla wafers

In a large bowl, blend cream cheese and powdered sugar. Add pie filling and spices; blend until smooth. Serve with small cookies for dipping. Makes 7 cups.

Sugared Pumpkin Seeds

Fill small treat bags to give as party favors.

1 c. pumpkin seeds
1 T. butter, melted
1 T. sugar

1/2 to 1 t. cinnamon
1/4 t. nutmeg
1/8 t. allspice

Rinse pumpkin seeds and pat dry; toss with butter, sugar and spices. Spread on a lightly greased baking sheet . Bake at 300 degrees for 45 to 60 minutes, turning occasionally, until crunchy and golden. Makes one cup.

Variation: Cajun Spiced Pumpkin Seeds:

1 c. pumpkin seeds
1 T. butter, melted
1/4 t. Worcestershire sauce

3/4 to 1 t. Cajun seasoning
1/8 t. paprika
1/8 t. salt

Prepare as above.

"Mauled" Apple Cider

A spicy hot beverage that mummies will love...daddies too!

2 qts. apple cider or apple juice	12 whole cloves
1/4 c. sugar	6 whole allspice
	4 4-inch cinnamon sticks

Combine all ingredients in a large saucepan. Over low heat, heat to boiling. Boil 3 to 5 minutes; remove and discard spices. Serve hot. Makes 16 servings.

Black Lagoon Punch

Surround the punch bowl with unearthly green glow necklaces.

.13-oz. env. unsweetened grape drink mix	2 c. sugar
.13-oz. env. unsweetened orange drink mix	3 qts. water
	1-ltr. bottle ginger ale, chilled

In a pitcher, stir together drink mixes, sugar and water until dissolved; chill. At serving time, pour into a punch bowl; add ginger ale. Makes 32 servings.

Create a creepy ice ring for your punch bowl! Fill a ring mold 1/3 full with green citrus soda. Freeze, then arrange gummy critters or plastic bugs on the ice. Fill ring 3/4 full and return to freezer. Run hot water over mold for just a second to unmold. How icky!

Monstrous Main Dishes

Thrift-store lanterns and hurricane globes make wonderful Halloween party lighting...the shabbier, the better! Arrange in a large table-top grouping and twine twinkling white lights inside.

Pumpkin Eater's Stew

A hearty beef stew, served in a fun way.

2 lbs. stew beef, cubed
3 T. oil, divided
1 c. water
3 potatoes, peeled and cubed
4 carrots, peeled and sliced
4 cloves garlic, minced
1 onion, chopped
6 cubes beef bouillon
1/2 t. pepper
14-1/2 oz. can diced tomatoes
10 to 12-lb. pumpkin, top and seeds removed

In a large saucepan over medium heat, brown beef in 2 tablespoons oil. Add remaining ingredients except tomatoes and pumpkin. Bring to a boil; reduce heat, cover and simmer for 2 hours. Stir in tomatoes. Spoon stew into pumpkin; set in a heavy baking pan. Brush remaining oil over pumpkin. Bake at 325 degrees for 2 hours, until pumpkin is tender. Scoop out some pumpkin with each serving. Makes 8 servings.

Hungry Monster Sandwich

Feeds one monster...or 12 to 14 mere mortals!

1 extra-long or 2 regular loaves Italian bread
8-oz. pkg. cream cheese, softened
1 c. shredded Cheddar cheese
3/4 c. green onion, chopped
1/4 c. mayonnaise
1 T. Worcestershire sauce
1 lb. sliced deli ham
1 lb. sliced deli roast beef
1/2 c. sliced dill pickles

Cut bread in half lengthwise; hollow out. Set aside. Combine cream cheese, Cheddar cheese, onion, mayonnaise and Worcestershire sauce; spread over both halves of bread. Layer ham, beef and pickles on bottom half of bread; press on top half. Wrap in plastic wrap; refrigerate for at least 2 hours. Cut into 1-1/2 to 2-inch slices. Makes 12 to 14 servings.

Roasted Hobgoblin Heads

Choose nice rounded peppers for the best heads.

6 green peppers, tops
  removed
1 lb. ground beef, browned
1-1/2 c. prepared rice
2 8-oz. cans tomato sauce,
  divided
1 T. Worcestershire sauce

1 T. dried, minced onion
1/4 t. garlic powder
salt and pepper to taste
1 t. Italian seasoning
12 spears asparagus
12 stuffed green olives
6 pimento strips

Arrange peppers in a greased 13"x9" baking pan. Combine beef, rice, one can tomato sauce, Worcestershire, onion, garlic powder, salt and pepper. Fill peppers evenly. Mix remaining sauce and Italian seasoning; spoon over peppers. Insert 2 asparagus spears in each pepper. Bake at 350 degrees for one hour, spooning sauce over top every 15 minutes. With a knife tip, cut 2 X's for "eyes" in each pepper; insert olives. Cut mouth slits and insert pimento "tongues." Serves 6.

Hocus-Pocus Enchiladas

So delicious, they'll disappear before your eyes!

8-oz. pkg. cream cheese,
  softened and divided
1/2 c. green onion, sliced
2 c. shredded Mexican-blend
  cheese
2 4-oz. cans diced green chiles,
  drained

1/2 t. ground cumin
3 eggs, beaten
1 T. oil
12 corn tortillas
2 8-oz. jars enchilada sauce
Garnish: 4-1/4 oz. can sliced
  black olives, drained

Combine half of cream cheese and onion in a small bowl; blend and set aside. Beat together shredded cheese, remaining cream cheese, chiles and cumin. Mix in eggs; set aside. Heat oil in a skillet; warm tortillas one at a time. Top each tortilla with 2 tablespoons shredded cheese mixture; roll up. Arrange, seam-side down, in a greased 13"x9" baking pan. Top with sauce. Bake at 350 degrees for 20 minutes, until hot. Dollop with cream cheese mixture; top with olives. Serves 6.

Monstrous Main Dishes

Creepy laughter, groaning ghosts, crashing thunder, rattling chains... don't forget to pick up a CD or tape of scary sounds! Or grab a tape recorder and let the kids create their own spooky soundtrack.

Whip up some creepy croutons for soups...use ghost or pumpkin cookie cutters to cut shapes out of sliced bread. Brush with olive oil, sprinkle with herbs and bake at 350 degrees for just a few minutes to crisp.

Bubbling Cauldron Soup

Serve from a black cast iron pot.

1/2 c. onion, chopped
2 green onions, chopped
1 T. butter
1 T. green chiles, diced
4 14-1/2 oz. cans chicken
  broth

1-1/2 lbs. sweet potatoes,
  peeled and cubed
2 c. cooked turkey, cubed
salt and pepper to taste
2 c. frozen corn

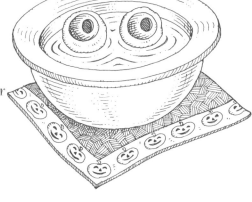

In a large saucepan over medium heat, sauté onions until tender. Add remaining ingredients except corn. Cover and simmer over low heat for 30 minutes, or until sweet potatoes are tender. Stir in corn; cook until heated through. Makes 8 to 10 servings.

L'eek! Soup

Warm up chilly trick-or-treaters with a cup of this soup.

4 leeks, sliced 1/4-inch thick
2 T. olive oil
4 russet potatoes, peeled
  and cubed
5 c. water
1 t. salt

1/2 t. pepper
8-oz. pkg. cream cheese,
  cubed
1/2 c. milk
Garnish: chopped fresh
  chives, crispy bacon

In a large saucepan over medium heat, sauté leeks in oil until tender. Add potatoes, water, salt and pepper; cover. Bring to boil; reduce heat and simmer for 15 to 20 minutes, until potatoes are tender. Cool 10 minutes; purée in batches in a blender. Return to saucepan. Whisk in cream cheese, a few cubes at a time; cook and stir over medium heat until melted. Add milk and heat through. Garnish as desired. Makes 8 servings.

Barbecued Worms on a Bun

Ewwww! So gross, the kids will love 'em!

4 hot dogs
1/2 to 3/4 c. barbecue sauce

4 hamburger buns, split
and toasted

Halve each hot dog lengthwise; slice each half into 3 to 4 thin strips. Place in a medium saucepan; cover with water. Bring to a boil over medium heat and cook for 4 to 5 minutes. Drain hot dogs well; return to saucepan. Stir in sauce over low heat until warmed through. Spoon onto buns. Serves 4.

Cheesy Apple Grillwitch

Your guests will be "goblin" these up!

8 slices cinnamon-raisin bread
4 slices American cheese
1 McIntosh apple, cored, peeled and
thinly sliced

8 t. butter, softened

For each sandwich, top one bread slice with a cheese slice, one-quarter of the apple slices and another bread slice. Spread butter thinly over outsides of sandwich. On a griddle over medium heat, cook until golden on both sides. Slice into halves. Makes 4 sandwiches.

Monstrous Main Dishes

Gather bouquets of fake flowers and a garland for the mantel...spray with flat black paint. On the front door, hang a black-sprayed wreath with a ribbon marked "Rest in Peace." Eerie!

A Halloween
Riddle...

Q: Why don't
mummies go
on vacation?

A: Because
they're afraid
they'll relax
and unwind!

Buggy Snack Cake

Never fear...the "bugs" are really raisins!

15-oz. can pumpkin
1 c. sugar
1 c. brown sugar, packed
1/2 c. butter, melted
4 eggs
2 t. vanilla extract
1-1/2 c. all-purpose flour
2-1/2 t. pumpkin pie spice

1 t. baking powder
1/2 t. baking soda
1/4 t. salt
1 c. raisins
1/2 c. chopped walnuts
16-oz. can cream cheese
    frosting

Blend pumpkin, sugars, butter, eggs and vanilla in a
large bowl with an electric mixer on medium speed.
Combine dry ingredients in a small bowl; stir into
pumpkin mixture. Add raisins and nuts. Pour
into a greased 13"x9" baking pan. Bake at
350 degrees for 35 to 40 minutes, until a toothpick
tests clean. Cool. Frost; let stand until set. Cut into
squares. Makes 2 to 3 dozen.

Cream-Filled Witches' Hats

*Short on time? Fill the hats with creamy chocolate whipped
topping instead.*

1-3/4 c. whipping cream, divided
6-oz. pkg. milk chocolate chips
4 1-oz. sqs. semi-sweet baking
    chocolate, chopped
1/2 t. shortening

12 chocolate-coated ice cream
    cones
12 thin chocolate wafer cookies
Garnish: candy sprinkles

Bring 1/2 cup cream to a boil in a saucepan; remove from
heat. Stir in chips until smooth; spoon into a bowl. Let cool,
stirring occasionally. Beat remaining cream with an electric
mixer on high speed until stiff peaks form; fold into
chocolate mixture. Chill. Melt baking chocolate and
shortening on high for one to 2 minutes; stir. Dip tips of
cones into chocolate, then into sprinkles. Chill until set.
To serve, spoon cream into cones; set each on a
cookie. Serves 12.

Scaredy Cat Cookies

Crushed candies create glowing green or yellow eyes!

1 c. butter, softened
1/2 c. sugar
2 egg yolks
1 t. vanilla extract

2-1/2 c. all-purpose flour
green or yellow hard
candies, crushed

With an electric mixer on medium speed, blend butter
and sugar until smooth. Beat in egg yolks and vanilla;
stir in flour until well mixed. Roll out dough, one-half
at a time, 1/4-inch thick on a floured surface. Cut out
with cat face cookie cutter; cut out "eyes" in each with a
mini cookie cutter or kn ⁇ tip. Arrange on a parchment
paper-covered baki ⁇ Bake at 300 degrees until
golden, about ⁇ Sprinkle crushed candies
into eye ⁇ ntil candies are melted,
ab⁇ ndies harden; finish
⁇ t 2 dozen.

Forgotten Ghosts

Lighter-than-air meringues...oh-so-easy ⁇

3 egg whites, at room
  temperature
1/4 t. cream of tartar
3/4 c. sugar

1 t. vanilla or pepp⁇
  extract
Garnish: decorating g⁇

Combine egg whites and cream of tartar in a mixing
bowl. Beat with an electric mixer on high speed until
soft peaks form. Beat in sugar 2 tablespoons at a time,
until stiff peaks form. Add extract. Spoon into a large
plastic zipping bag; snip off one tip of bag. Pipe one-inch
swirls, as for soft-serve ice cream, onto parchment
paper-lined baking sheets. Place in a preheated
200-degree oven; bake for one hour. Turn off oven; leave
cookies in oven for one additional hour, until crisp. With
decorating gel, pipe "eyes" on cookies. Makes 3 dozen.

Devilish Desserts

Mold a funny or freaky face of gelatin, ice cream or even ice for your party buffet! Simply turn a hard plastic mask face-down, line with plastic wrap and fill as desired. Chill, then turn out onto a platter and peel off plastic wrap.

Sorcerer's Caramel Apples

The caramel almost cooks itself!

2 14-oz. pkgs. caramels, unwrapped
1/4 c. water
8 apples
8 wooden skewers

Garnish: candy sprinkles, mini candy-coated chocolates, chopped nuts

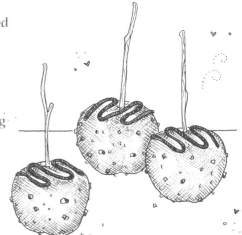

Combine caramels and water in a slow cooker. Cover and cook on high for one to 1-1/2 hours, stirring frequently, until melted. Insert skewers into apples. Dip each apple into caramel, turning to coat. Set apples to dry on lightly greased wax paper. When partially set, roll in toppings as desired. Makes 8 apples.

I Scream Pumpkin Pie

Devilishly delicious!

1 pt. vanilla ice cream, softened
9-inch graham cracker crust
15-oz. can pumpkin
3/4 c. sugar

2 t. pumpkin pie spice
1/2 t. salt
8-oz. container frozen whipped topping, thawed and divided

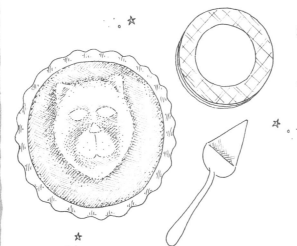

Spoon ice cream into crust; cover and freeze until solid. Blend together pumpkin, sugar, spice and salt; fold in one cup whipped topping. Spoon over frozen ice cream layer; cover and freeze until solid. One hour before serving time, move from freezer to refrigerator to soften. Spread remaining topping over pie. Serves 8 to 10.

All Hallow's Eve Poke Cake

Garnish this tasty chocolate and orange marble cake with candy pumpkins.

18-1/4 oz. pkg. fudge marble
  cake mix
2 3-oz. pkgs. orange gelatin
  mix
1 c. boiling water
1/2 c. cold water

1/2 c. butter, softened
3-1/2 c. powdered sugar
1/3 c. baking cocoa
1/4 c. milk
1 t. vanilla extract

Prepare cake mix as package directs; bake in a greased 13"x9" baking pan. Cool on a wire rack for one hour. In a small bowl, dissolve gelatin in boiling water; add cold water. With a wooden spoon handle, poke holes in cake 2-inches apart. Slowly pour gelatin over cake; chill for 2 to 3 hours. Blend butter, powdered sugar, cocoa, milk and vanilla until smooth; spread over cake. Keep chilled. Makes 15 servings.

Trick-or-Treat Popcorn Balls

Makes a LOT...you'll need either a helper or a magic wand! Add a few drops of red and yellow food coloring for pumpkin-orange balls.

5 qts. popped popcorn
3/4 c. light corn syrup
1/4 c. butter
2 t. cold water

1 t. vanilla or cinnamon
  extract
2-3/4 c. powdered sugar
1 c. mini marshmallows

Place popcorn in a very large bowl or roasting pan; remove any unpopped kernels and set aside. Combine remaining ingredients in a saucepan over medium heat. Cook and stir until mixture comes to a boil. Carefully pour hot mixture over popcorn, coating each kernel. Spray hands with non-stick vegetable spray and quickly shape into balls. Makes about 1-1/2 dozen.

Mini pumpkins lit with tea candles occupy a 3-tiered stand. Hollowing out the pumpkins from the bottom not only preserves the stems, but allows you to set them directly over the votive.

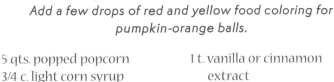

Going for an eerie atmosphere at your front entranceway? Decorate with ghostly white Lumina pumpkins for a totally different effect than friendly orange pumpkins.

Spooky Skull Cupcakes

What fun! Oh-so-easy to do too.

18-1/2 oz. pkg. white cake mix
12 marshmallows
16-oz. can vanilla frosting

Garnish: mini chocolate-covered mints, chocolate chips, slivered almonds

Prepare cake mix as package directs; bake in 24 muffin cups lined with white paper liners. Cool. Cut each marshmallow in half from top to bottom. Carefully pull each paper liner partially away from cupcake; tuck a marshmallow half between liner and cupcake to create "jaw" of skull. Spread frosting over cupcake and marshmallow. Add mints dotted with white frosting for "eyes," a chocolate chip for a "nose" and slivered almond "teeth." Makes 2 dozen.

Eerie Ooze Cupcakes

Tint the ooze blood-red if you dare!

18-1/2 oz. pkg. devil's food cake mix
8-oz. pkg. cream cheese, softened

1 egg
1/3 c. sugar
several drops green food coloring

Prepare cake mix as directed on package; set aside. Blend cream cheese, egg and sugar; add food coloring to desired shade. Place 24 paper cupcake liners in muffin cups; fill 1/2 full with cake batter. Place one teaspoon filling in center of each (batter will rise to surround filling). Bake at 350 degrees for 25 minutes. Makes 2 dozen.

Fire Ant Fudge

Place squares in Halloween-printed paper candy cups.

2 6-oz. pkgs. white baking
    chocolate, chopped
3/4 c. sweetened con-
    densed milk
1 T. orange zest

1 c. toasted almonds,
    coarsely chopped
1/2 c. sweetened, dried
    cranberries

Place chocolate and condensed milk in a microwave-
safe container. Microwave on medium for 2 to
3 minutes; stir until completely melted. Stir in zest,
nuts and cranberries. Spread in an aluminum foil-lined
8"x8" baking pan. Chill for 2 hours. Turn fudge out of pan;
peel off foil and cut into small squares. Store, tightly
covered, in refrigerator. Makes 4 dozen pieces.

A Halloween
Riddle...

Q: When does
a skeleton
laugh?

A: When
something
tickles his
funny bone!

Candied Pumpkin

A deliciously different treat.

4 c. pumpkin, peeled and cut into
    1"x1-1/2" cubes
2-1/2 c. water

1 c. brown sugar, packed
1 c. raw or maple sugar

Combine pumpkin and water in a saucepan; bring to a boil. Reduce heat and
simmer, uncovered for 15 to 20 minutes, until tender. Drain, reserving 1-1/2 cups of
liquid in pan; set aside pumpkin. Add brown sugar to reserved liquid; stir over low
heat until dissolved. Return pumpkin to pan. Slowly bring to a boil; reduce heat
and simmer, uncovered, for 15 minutes. Remove from heat and let stand overnight.
Next day, return mixture to a boil; simmer for
5 minutes. Remove pumpkin pieces with a
slotted spoon; place on a wire rack set on
a baking sheet. Bake at 170 degrees for
3 to 4 hours, until dry. Roll pumpkin
pieces in raw or maple sugar. Store
loosely in a dry, cool place.
Makes 2 pounds.

Eerie Edible Crafts

Pop brightly colored face masks over water-filled glass vases or Mason jars...drop in tealights for a mysterious candle glow!

Swamp Dirt Cups

Kids will giggle when they see these!

2 c. milk
3.9-oz. pkg. instant chocolate pudding mix
8-oz. container frozen whipped topping, thawed
16-oz. pkg. chocolate sandwich cookies, crushed and divided

8 9-oz. clear plastic cups
Garnish: gummy worms, gummy frogs, toasted coconut, candy pebbles, granola

Whisk milk and pudding mix together; let stand for 5 minutes. Fold in topping and half the cookie crumbs; set aside. Spoon one tablespoon remaining crumbs into each cup; fill 3/4 full with pudding. Sprinkle with remaining crumbs; chill at least one hour. Garnish as desired with gummy creatures, coconut "dead grass," candy pebbles and granola "gravel." Makes 8.

Witch's Delight Snack Mix

A fun jar gift for Halloween! Attach a label listing all the creepy ingredients in your most spidery handwriting.

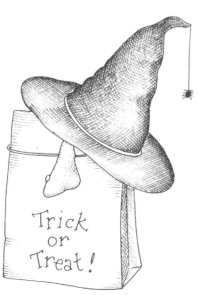

Trick or Treat!

1/2 c. wild berries (red jelly beans)
1/2 c. owl rings (doughnut-shaped oat cereal)
1/2 c. colored flies (candy-coated chocolates)
1/2 c. butterfly wings (corn chips)
1/2 c. cobwebs (sweetened flaked coconut)

1/2 c. ants (raisins)
1/2 c. earthworms (chow mein noodles)
1/2 c. squirrels' nuts (peanuts)
1/2 c. bat bones (mini pretzels)
1/2 c. birdseed (sunflower kernels)

Mix all ingredients together in a large bowl; store in an airtight container. Makes about 5 to 6 cups.

Monster Hands

Great party favors...fill up a punch bowl with hands "crawling" over the edge!

disposable clear plastic
   kitchen gloves
popped popcorn

candy corn
curling ribbon
plastic spider rings

For each "hand," place a candy corn "fingernail" in each fingertip of a glove. Pack glove tightly with popped corn, starting with the fingers. Tie top of glove with curling ribbon. Slip a spider ring onto one finger of the "hand." Make as many as you like!

A tried & true party game... start a ghost story circle. Sit in a circle and begin telling a scary ghost story. Each person adds to the story until it reaches a surprise ending!

Giant Bugs

Don't worry, they won't bite...you bite them!

12-oz. pkg. melting chocolate, chopped
16-oz. pkg. peanut butter
   sandwich cookies

64 mini pretzel twists
4 t. mini candy-coated
   chocolates

Place chocolate in a microwave-safe container; microwave on high until melted. Stir until until smooth. Use tongs to dip cookies into chocolate; set on a wax paper-lined baking sheet. Cut pretzels into curved C-shaped pieces for legs and antennae. With dabs of melted chocolate, attach 3 pretzel pieces on each side of a cookie for legs; arrange another 2 pieces at front for antennae. Add candy-coated chocolates for eyes. Let stand for 10 minutes until chocolate sets up. Makes about 2-1/2 dozen.

A Halloween Riddle...

Q: How do you mend a broken Jack-'O-Lantern?

A: With a pumpkin patch!

Masquerade Cookies

Make your own mask cookie patterns! Just trace around real half-masks on cardboard and cut out.

18-oz. pkg. refrigerated gingerbread or sugar cookie dough

Garnish: edible glitter, small candies

Roll out dough 3/8-inch thick on a floured surface. Cut out cookies; arrange on parchment paper-lined baking sheets. Bake at 350 degrees for 10 to 12 minutes, until golden. Cool. Frost cookies with a small spatula or new paintbrush; decorate as desired. Makes 6 to 8.

Royal Icing:

1/2 c. pasteurized egg whites
1/2 t. cream of tartar
16-oz. pkg. powdered sugar

several drops food coloring

Combine all ingredients except coloring in a large bowl. Beat for several minutes with an electric mixer on high speed until smooth. Divide into small bowls and color as desired.

Crispy Jack-'O-Lanterns

Make pumpkin pops with the same recipe! Simply form 2-inch balls of the cereal mixture around treat sticks.

3 T. butter
10-1/2 oz. pkg. mini marshmallows
20 drops yellow food coloring

5 drops red food coloring
6 c. crispy rice cereal
Garnish: black licorice laces, chocolate chips

Melt butter in a large saucepan over low heat. Add marshmallows; cook and stir until melted. Add food coloring; remove from heat. Add cereal; stir until well coated. Cool slightly. Lightly grease hands and a one-cup measure; use hands to press mixture into cup. Turn out immediately; form into a pumpkin shape. Press thumb into top to hollow out. Insert short pieces of licorice for handles; press in chocolate chips to create faces. Set on wax paper for 30 minutes. Makes 6.

Mummies' Fingers

Frightful, delightful digits!

6-oz. pkg. white chocolate
  chips
8 pretzel rods, broken in
  half

1 t. baking cocoa

Place chocolate chips in a microwave-safe container. Microwave on high for one to 2 minutes, stirring every 15 seconds, just until melted. With tongs, dip pretzel halves into chocolate; place on a wax paper-lined baking sheet. Spoon remaining chocolate into a small plastic zipping bag; snip off a small corner. Pipe lines over pretzels to form "wrappings." Chill until set, about 5 minutes. Sprinkle ends lightly with cocoa "dust." Makes 16.

Eerie Edible Crafts

Drape your dessert table in edible spider-webs...strands of cotton candy!

Magic Stirring Spoons

Dress up your spoons...drizzle with melted candy coating disks in pumpkin orange or witchy purple.

12-oz. pkg. semi-sweet
  chocolate chips
2 t. shortening

3 to 4 doz. plastic spoons
Garnish: small candies

Place chocolate chips in a microwave-safe container. Microwave on medium for 2 minutes, or until melted, stirring every 30 seconds. Add shortening; stir gently. Dip bowls of spoons into chocolate mixture; place on a wax paper-lined baking sheet. Arrange candies on spoons as desired while chocolate is still soft; cool completely. Wrap spoons individually in plastic wrap. Makes 3 to 4 dozen.

Turn apples into mini candle holders...just hollow out, slip a votive inside and float along with some colorful leaves in an old-fashioned copper washtub.

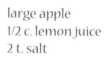

Shrunken Apple Heads

Scatter them around the buffet table!

large apple
1/2 c. lemon juice
2 t. salt

Optional: whole cloves, uncooked rice

Peel apple without coring. Stir lemon juice and salt together; dip apple to prevent browning. Carve out eyes with tip of a potato peeler; use a small knife to roughly shape nose, mouth and ears. If desired, press in cloves for eyes and rice for teeth. Leave on a wire rack in a warm, dry place for about 2 weeks, continuing to carve face as it dries. Drying process can be speeded up by placing in a 200-degree oven for 4 to 5 hours, then air-drying for 2 days.

Haunted Gingerbread House

"Who's that nibbling on my house?" said the witch.

empty milk cartons, cereal
   or other food boxes
masking tape or hot glue
cardboard square

Royal Icing (page 20)
graham crackers
assorted candies, pretzels,
   cookies, cereals

Arrange several cartons or boxes to form a house shape. Join with tape or hot glue; attach to cardboard square for a base. Use Royal Icing to cover walls of house with graham crackers (you may need more than one batch of icing). Decorate house and base as you like, using icing to attach decorations. Use your own imagination...how about candy pumpkins piled in the yard, with marshmallow ghosts at the door?

Boo-tiful Buckets

First stop, a paint store to buy buckets. Next stop, a craft store...to see what fun trims they have!

new white paper paint
   buckets
acrylic craft paints
18-inch length craft cord
craft glue

Decorations: Halloween-
   shape foam craft
   cut-outs, half-masks,
   large wiggle eyes,
   pompom cord, fringe

Paint buckets as desired with craft paint. Punch a hole at top on each side; insert cord handle and knot on outside. Trim as desired. Some ideas:

- Arrange foam cut-outs of pumpkins, bats, ghosts or other seasonal shapes around bucket.
- Glue a half-mask on either side of bucket; slide wiggle eyes behind eye holes and glue.
- Paint on stripes or polka dots. Glue pompoms or fringe along edge of bucket.

Drive guests batty...cut out flying bats from sheets of black plastic film and simply smooth in place on mirrors or windows.

Sleepy Hollow Treat Tree

A fun way to display candy-filled paper cones...send one home with each guest as party favors!

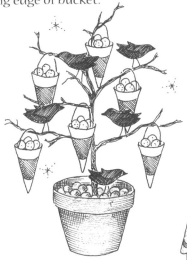

black acrylic spray paint
leafless tree branch
large terra cotta pot
pebbles or sand
seasonal scrapbooking or
   wrapping paper
narrow ribbon or rick-rack

craft glue
wrapped candies
Optional: mini twinkle
   lights, artificial black
   crows, black curling
   ribbon

Paint branch and pot with spray paint; let dry. Fill pot with pebbles or sand and "plant" tree firmly. Set aside. To make treat cones, cut paper into 12-inch diameter circles; fold and cut into quarters. Roll each quarter into a cone; tape to secure. Decorate cones as desired; attach ribbon or rick-rack handles with glue. Trim tree as desired with twinkle lights, crows and strands of black curling ribbon; hang cones from tree.

Frightfully Fun Crafts

Shake up your pumpkin display! Winter squashes come in many sizes, shapes and colors...they're as easy to carve as pumpkins. Green kabocha, bumpy gray Hubbard squash and mini sweet dumplings all make fun Jack-'O-Lanterns.

Trick-or-Treat Jar

The perfect place to stash Halloween candy!

vintage seasonal postcard
cardstock
craft glue
large glass apothecary jar
 with lid

Optional: glitter, craft
 paint

Make a color photocopy of Halloween-themed postcard and glue to cardstock; let dry. Cut out postcard with decorative-edged scissors; glue to front of jar. If desired, decorate postcard with glitter; write "My Treats... Everyone Else Keep Out!" on jar with craft paint.

Candy Corn Cups

Oh-so-easy table favors to fill with treats.

mini terra cotta pots
paint brush

orange, yellow and white
 acrylic craft paint

Paint top third of pots (rims) with yellow paint; let dry. Paint middle third orange and bottom third white.

Pumpkin Piñata

Fill the piñata with vintage-style candies like wax lips, root beer barrels, circus peanuts and bubble gum. Your grown-up party guests will feel like kids again!

newspaper, torn into
   strips
pre-mixed wallpaper paste
large round balloon

acrylic craft paints
heavy jute or cord
assorted candies

Dip strips of newspaper into wallpaper paste; smooth over inflated balloon to cover completely. Make 4 to 6 layers; let dry in a warm place for several days. Cut a hole in top; pop and remove balloon. Allow to finish drying inside. Paint orange; paint on a Jack-'O-Lantern face. Attach jute or cord for hanging to either side of hole. Fill with candies.

A Halloween Riddle...

Q: What has fur, howls at the moon and is easy to clean?

A: A wash & werewolf!

Who Are You? Face Masks

Fun to tuck into a vase as a table decoration...keep some on hand for guests who arrive without a mask!

photos of famous people
   or Halloween
   characters
thin cardboard
craft glue

paint stirring sticks
hot glue
Optional: craft paint,
   glitter

Take your chosen photos to a copy shop. Have them enlarged to the size of an actual face (about 8-inches high) and copied in color. Glue to cardboard backing using craft glue spread thinly. When dry, cut around faces; cut out eye holes. Attach a stirring stick holder to the back of each mask using hot glue. If you like, decorate sticks with paint or glitter.

Host a Halloween Party!

Copy, color & cut out this ready-to-go invitation. Just fill in your information and mail!

HAPPY HALLOWEEN!
You're Invited:

What: _____

When: _____

Where: _____

R.S.V.P.: _____

Eat, Drink & Be Scary!

To: _____

From: _____

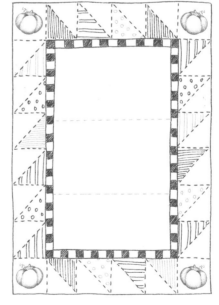

Copy these gift tags and glue onto pretty cardstock to attach to treat bags!

Whoooo to invite?

Make your guest list here:

_____

_____

_____

_____

_____

_____

_____

_____

_____

_____